The Monday Morning Minute

A One Year
Weekly Motivational Journal

Sonja W. Bachus

The Monday Morning Minute

Copyright © 2022 Sonja W. Bachus

Published by Sonja W. Bachus

ISBN: 979-8-9863377-2-2 (Paperback Edition)
ISBN: 979-8-9863377-4-6 (Hardcover Edition)
ISBN: 979-8-9863377-3-9 (Ebook Edition)

Printed in the United States of America

Introduction

The Monday Morning Minute was first developed in January 2020 as a weekly motivational message for the healthcare organization I led from April 2019 through October 2022. After several team members mentioned they shared many of these weekly posts with their families and friends, I set out to do the same by sharing the weekly Monday Morning Minute on my Instagram pages: @TheMondayMorningMinute and @SonjaWBachus.

The Monday Morning Minute is intended to start your week off with motivating inspiration. Some weeks the intention is to inspire you to pursue your goals and dreams and some weeks are reminders to intentionally care for yourselves and even others in the process. The purpose is not to mix signals, but to ensure that the hard work, resilience and grit required to be at your best to achieve your goals is balanced with mindfulness and self-care.

Because I have an affinity for quotes (I have them everywhere in both print and digital formats), each Monday Morning Minute shares a motivational concept and at least one quote that you can carry forward into your week. This journal is also created to give you some space to write down your own thoughts, document your goals, and/or add your favorite quotes on the week's subject as you begin and end each week.

Since we are all so busy, each week's commentary is meant to be read in a just a few moments; hence the title: "The Monday Morning Minute".

It is my hope that this journal helps you to set a positive and productive tone for each week and that you will also take time to reflect at the end of each week on how you may have utilized the weekly message or quote.

Please follow me on Instagram at @TheMondayMorningMinute or @SonjaWBachus.

Dedication

This journal is dedicated to my former team members at Greater Baden Medical Services whose acceptance and appreciation of my weekly messages inspired me to continue writing each week and to my family and friends who supported my desire to bring motivation and inspiration to the worlds beyond my immediate circle.

1

DATE:_____

    Blaine Lee, author of "The Power Principle: Influence with Honor" said "When people honor each other, there is a trust established that leads to synergy, interdependence, and deep respect. Both parties make decisions and choices based on what is right, what is best, and what is valued most highly." Begin by eliminating judgement and honoring yourself and your unique gifts to the world. Honor others regardless of your similarities or differences. There are times when you must look past the present moment and the actions or reaction of others because some are happy, yet some are facing traumas we know nothing about. Know that you are an amazing, talented being. You are more than your level of education. You are more than your job. You are more than any past circumstance. You are daughter, son, sister, brother, parent, aunt, uncle, cousin, musician, artist, healer, poet, walker, runner, yogi, athlete, preacher, teacher. The list goes on and on. Most importantly you are a human being fully capable of love and light and the capacity to give honor to yourself, to others, even to moments in time. You are uniquely and brilliantly you and so much more. Phenomenally, you share that love and light again and again each day. To honor yourself and others is powerful! Live in and give honor ALWAYS.

Monday Morning Minute:

_____

_____

_____

_____

_____

_____

_____

_____

_____

Friday Follow-up:

_____

_____

_____

_____

_____

_____

_____

_____

2

Remember this: "This push and pull, yin and yang world can isolate us at times— but that should not insulate us from the needs of others. Indeed, the grace that we give, the help that turns to hope, and encouragement that empowers us that we're never alone." -Gary Burnison. Each day we encounter and interact with others; in our families, as we are driving on the road, those who answer at businesses we call on the phone or visit in person, those we work with and more. Everyone has something going on outside of the immediate interaction. Some have an unpaid utility bill or rent, some have a medical condition they just can't seem to get under control, some can't afford medications for those conditions, some have a family member with a catastrophic illness or a child struggling in school or life, some are caught in a bad relationship, and some have an undiagnosed or unmanaged mental illness. We don't always know the SOMETHING. Simply try to imagine what they might be facing that you know nothing about. Take a moment to just imagine they need the same grace you sometimes need. Even when you think your action or reaction goes unnoticed and you don't know if it helps them, most times it WILL help you. Give a little grace.

Monday Morning Minute:

_____

_____

_____

_____

_____

_____

_____

_____

_____

Friday Follow-up:

_____

_____

_____

_____

_____

_____

_____

_____

_____

3

What is your purpose?

Why do you do what you do on a daily basis? It's not that difficult to describe WHAT we do and/or HOW we do it. However, getting to the WHY is sometimes more difficult. It takes some reflection and possibly even deep soul searching to establish our WHY. Our why helps us to define our true purpose.

Merriam-Webster defines purpose in the following three ways:

- the reason why something is done or used: the aim or intention of something
- the feeling of being determined to do or achieve
- the aim or goal of a person: what a person is trying to do, become, etc.

Developing a personal purpose statement will provide you with clarity, define your direction and help you choose what you say yes or no to. You are here for a purpose. You HAVE purpose. What is YOUR unique purpose?

Monday Morning Minute:

_____

_____

_____

_____

_____

_____

_____

_____

Friday Follow-up:

_____

_____

_____

_____

_____

_____

_____

_____

DATE:_____

    The pandemic changed the world. If not before, we should now know how critical it is to pause. It is one of the lessons learned during the time most of us gained during the 2020 shutdown. Take advantage of the pause. This quote from Dave Hollis puts in perspective how we should be careful in how we come out of the pause the "shut down slow down" forced on us. "Let's remember who and what is important in our lives: In the rush to return to normal, use this time to consider which parts of normal are worth rushing back to. If things go back exactly as they were, we will have missed the opportunity to take the good from this bad." This world we live in can bring us so much joy yet can, in contrast, be quite challenging at times. Remember to be intentional in selecting when, where and how you expend your time and energy. Find ways to take the good from the bad, starting with the PAUSE.

Monday Morning Minute:

_____

_____

_____

_____

_____

_____

_____

_____

_____

Friday Follow-up:

_____

_____

_____

_____

_____

_____

_____

_____

_____

5

DATE:_____

"You will never reach your destination if you stop and throw stones at every dog that barks." -Winston Churchill. If recent years have taught us anything, taking time to carefully consider and decide what is truly important is one of the most important lessons we could have learned. We have also learned that we must keep moving forward no matter the circumstance. Progress requires dedicated focus and determination. If we allow every little background noise to distract us and get us off the path toward our goal, we risk missing the opportunity to reach the greatness we are destined for. Each of us are amazing individuals and only as limited as we allow ourselves to be. We have much to offer the world and our focus is a critical component of our ability to reach our full potential. Let nothing distract you or get in your way. Stay focused. What do you need to focus on; today, tomorrow, this week, this month, this year?

Monday Morning Minute:

_____

_____

_____

_____

_____

_____

_____

_____

_____

Friday Follow-up:

_____

_____

_____

_____

_____

_____

_____

_____

6

New ideas, change, innovation; we need them all to advance whether personally or professionally. We see often how quickly circumstances can change when well thought out risks are taken. Nearly every business and human on the face of the earth has had to face the uncomfortable truth that life as we knew it will never be the same again. From the federal government to state and local ones, businesses, schools, families and as individuals, we have had to continue attempting new and different ways to accomplish daily tasks and larger goals. Some attempts worked well and some not so much. The key is to keep going, trying new ways of getting things done and not staying stuck in the comfort zone. Service Merchandise, Blockbuster Video and Nokia are prime examples of businesses whose comfort zone led them to ruin. They did not move as the needs of the customer changed. Jeff Bezos, CEO of Amazon, one of the most successful businesses we know said, "If you do only the things you know are going to work, you're going to leave a lot on the table." Get out of your comfort zone, be creative and innovative to advance yourself and reach the goals. The possibilities are endless. Don't leave anything on the table. What possibility is waiting for you?

Monday Morning Minute:

_____

_____

_____

_____

_____

_____

_____

_____

Friday Follow-up:

_____

_____

_____

_____

_____

_____

_____

_____

7

"We delight in the beauty of the butterfly, but rarely admit the changes it has gone through to achieve that beauty." -Maya Angelou. The evolution of the butterfly from prickly, crawling caterpillar to soaring butterfly with beautiful wings is a fitting example of evolution and transformation. The path of transformation from average and ordinary to true greatness is not easy. There are roadblocks, stumbles, and setbacks. There are both challenges and triumphs. It gets uncomfortable at times. Like the transformation of the caterpillar to butterfly; any beautiful flower garden you've seen, has not only been nurtured with water and fertilizer, but the dirt has also been tilled with sharp tools, weeds have been pulled and leaves pruned. Still, the end result is beautiful and the sight worth the toil. What transformation are you ready for?

Monday Morning Minute:

_____

_____

_____

_____

_____

_____

_____

_____

Friday Follow-up:

_____

_____

_____

_____

_____

_____

_____

_____

8

"If you don't make time for your wellness, you will be forced to make time for your illness." -Anonymous. So many of us take care of others in many ways and do not make taking care of ourselves a priority. Only you can determine what brings balance to your life so be careful not to let others define what balance means to you. Balance for me is likely quite different from what works for you. What are you doing to take care of yourself? Eating healthier, getting exercise, practicing a morning or night meditation or prayer ritual, taking some quiet time for yourself or connecting with friends and family? When flight attendants review the safety precautions before takeoff, we are always reminded to put the oxygen mask on ourselves before we help anyone else in the event of an emergency. Remember to care for yourself to best care for others and prioritize care for yourself by building time to establish balance in your life.

Monday Morning Minute:

_____

_____

_____

_____

_____

_____

_____

_____

Friday Follow-up:

_____

_____

_____

_____

_____

_____

_____

_____

9

DATE:_____

My mother used to remind me frequently of the familiar saying, "Rome wasn't built in a day", when I would tell her about my work and how many things I was working to change, create or collaborate on all at one time. I'd say, "Mama I know that, but there is so much to be done I just have to tackle it all at once!" Then I heard the James Clear quote, "Rome wasn't built in a day, but they were laying bricks every hour." That energized me AND put things in perspective. Robert Collier's statement, "Success is the sum of small efforts repeated day in and day out", is similar in nature. I don't know about you, but I drive for big results and most of the time I want to see them as quickly as humanly possible. Through the years I have come to know that many results come from the small, repeated efforts, the laying of bricks daily. Know that every step toward a goal counts. Small savings add up to large sums. Small improvements will lead to amazing results over time. Are you stacking bricks every day? What efforts will you make to ensure your success?

Monday Morning Minute:

_____

_____

_____

_____

_____

_____

_____

_____

Friday Follow-up:

_____

_____

_____

_____

_____

_____

_____

_____

10

Mario Andretti once said, "if everything seems under control, you're not going fast enough." You may be thinking this journal is full of contradictions, yet it is intentionally created to inspire you to committing to and reaching your goals, pressing toward success while learning to develop the tools that allow you to create balance, calm and positivity in your life. You can best believe that the most successful people you see have developed both intense drive and their required balance in the precise proportions that fit their needs.

One of Merriam-Webster's definitions of accelerate is "to hasten the progress or development of". What's lagging in your life right now? Have you become too comfortable with allowing your projects, goals and dreams to linger? What do you want to do that you have not done? A new job, more education, a business you've always dreamed of, a book you've had in your head and/or heart... If you have been stagnant or just going through the motions of everyday life and work, what is holding you back? Is it fear, lack of time, resources, or support? Whatever holds you back, it's time to push past the barriers and pursue your goal. Don't be afraid of not being in control of every single step. If you plan to win, you must move. If there is something you wish to accomplish, accelerate!

Monday Morning Minute:

_____

_____

_____

_____

_____

_____

_____

_____

_____

Friday Follow-up:

_____

_____

_____

_____

_____

_____

_____

_____

_____

11

"We humans have lost the wisdom of genuinely resting and relaxing. We worry too much. We don't allow our bodies to heal, and we don't allow our minds and hearts to heal. -Thich Nhat Hanh. Being self-aware, understanding who we are and our needs is vitally important to continued self-improvement and also a balanced life. This includes knowing when we need to take a break. For those of us who live to achieve, it is extremely difficult to stop that "work, hustle, succeed" and then do it all over again cycle. Sometimes it's "work, hustle, fail" and then the work and hustle hit overdrive to make up for the failure. I must admit I am quite guilty of these cycles. Watch for those signs. Be wise. Not just a wise spouse, parent, friend, leader or employee. Be wise enough to know your own needs and realize you owe it to yourself and those around you to rest, relax and, when needed, to heal.

Monday Morning Minute:

_____

_____

_____

_____

_____

_____

_____

Friday Follow-up:

_____

_____

_____

_____

_____

_____

_____

12

"You must do the things you think you cannot do." -Eleanor Roosevelt. According to the Merriam-Webster Dictionary, having tenacity means one is persistent in maintaining, adhering to, or seeking something valued or desired. Growth comes from stepping out of comfort zones, facing challenges, conquering fears, being bold, and at times taking the chance that no one else will understand or believe in, what you are dreaming of or planning. **Do it anyway!** Do not let anything hold you back. Take some time to think about just one thing you wish to do and have been putting off or maybe have been afraid to do. You **ARE** smart enough. You **DO** have what it takes. You **CAN** do it. You **WILL** find the money. Whatever you are thinking of may not be easy, yet my guess is that it will be worth the time and effort in the long run if it really is important to you. What is the thing you think you cannot do? It is time do it.

Monday Morning Minute:

_____

_____

_____

_____

_____

_____

_____

Friday Follow-up:

_____

_____

_____

_____

_____

_____

_____

13

"The pessimist sees difficulty in every opportunity. The optimist sees the opportunity in every difficulty." -Winston Churchill. Always, even when it's difficult to do so, look for the opportunities and possibilities. Look for what *can* happen, the YES... Problems are problems because we view them as such. The failure will come if that is what we look for instead of the success.

I happen to be both an optimist and a realist. Optimism allows seeing the possibilities in almost any situation. Realism allows seeing situations clearly and then balancing that positive outlook with the reality of whatever is being faced or what must be done. Even the most optimistic people I know, myself included, allow doubt to creep in from time to time and it quickly results in derailing the ability to see what CAN happen when seeing an exciting challenge to overcome and an opportunity to beat the odds. When I think about the power of perspective, I recall a pivotal moment during an extremely tough time in my life and career. I caught a glimpse of a small plaque on the cabinet in my office that simply states: "The best is yet to come." Even when you are unsure about the present or the future, remember it is your perspective that dictates, not necessarily the outcome, but how you manage through the challenges you may face. Evaluate your perspective.

Monday Morning Minute:

_____

_____

_____

_____

_____

_____

_____

_____

_____

Friday Follow-up:

_____

_____

_____

_____

_____

_____

_____

_____

_____

14

DATE:_____

    There is power in community. Henry Ford said, "Coming together is the beginning. Keeping together is progress. Working together is success." Community is built on the foundation of common goals and the recognition that none of us can do it all on our own. Communities care for, motivate and protect one another. When you see sports teams arise as champions, you are witnessing groups of individuals putting ego and pride aside for the good of the entire team, putting their best foot forward, utilizing all their natural and practiced talent in support of reaching that ultimate goal. They create an environment of community within their team. Their success relies on each one recognizing their role on the team and contributing while fully respecting the role of others. There are coaches, trainers, mentors, some even within the same positions doing their part and helping each other to excel. Their power of community allows for more consistent wins and support for one another when there is a loss. Who is your community? How do you honor your community?

Monday Morning Minute:

_____

_____

_____

_____

_____

_____

_____

_____

Friday Follow-up:

_____

_____

_____

_____

_____

_____

_____

_____

15

DATE:_____

We have endless opportunities to learn and grow. No matter the amount of education or years of experience we already have, there is always more to learn and ways to get better. We may mistakenly think we "know it all", believing our way is the best or only way. There is no limit to what can be accomplished when our self-awareness is at its highest and determination is put into action. Zig Ziglar said, "If you are willing to learn, no one can help you. If you are determined to learn, no one can stop you". The greatest leaders will consistently tell you their successes are built on learning daily and from nearly everyone they encounter. They read and they make time to think about what they learn so the new or expanded knowledge can be put into action in their daily activities. Be a continuous learner. Stay open and willing to learn and grow.

Monday Morning Minute:

_____

_____

_____

_____

_____

_____

_____

_____

Friday Follow-up:

_____

_____

_____

_____

_____

_____

_____

_____

16

DATE:_____

"Happiness is an attitude. We either make ourselves miserable, or happy and strong. The amount of work is the same." -Francesca Reigler. Our happiness is directly influenced by our own thoughts and choices. When I think of the similarities among some of the happiest people I know, the one trait they all possess is their deliberate choice to be happy and find the sunshine in any situation. They actively choose to not allow circumstances to make them miserable and, more importantly, they continue to share their happiness with others in spite of any issues they face. Some days and even some entire seasons of your life, everything will go just as planned. On the contrary, some days and seasons of life you may find yourself knocked down over and over. Some days the news of what is happening in the world around you will be terrible enough to bring you down. While you don't have to be happy about what is happening, you can choose to be happy in spite of the circumstance. Choose to be happy through both good and bad times. How will you choose happiness in your present circumstances?

Monday Morning Minute:

_____

_____

_____

_____

_____

_____

_____

Friday Follow-up:

_____

_____

_____

_____

_____

_____

_____

17

DATE:_____

The best way to find yourself is to lose yourself in the service of others. -Mahatma Gandhi. Service to others can be a source of great joy in our lives. As we give and serve, our own lives grow exponentially. Focusing on serving others helps us avoid becoming complacent, so concentrated on our daily routines, we forget how blessed and lucky we are to be able to serve others. Service is not always a monumental event. There is an opportunity in every human interaction. A kind word, a smile, an opened door and many other small gestures are acts of service that may impact another life in a way you did not imagine. Muhammad Ali said, "Service to others is the rent you pay for your room here on earth". Know that in serving others you will often find that you gain as much as those you are serving. Remember to recognize the importance of service. How do you serve?

Monday Morning Minute:

_____

_____

_____

_____

_____

_____

_____

_____

Friday Follow-up:

_____

_____

_____

_____

_____

_____

_____

_____

18

"Excellence is the gradual result of always striving to do better." -Pat Riley. Consistently operating with excellence can feel tedious. Taking short cuts or accomplishing tasks with minimum effort may allow us to get to the finish line faster, yet, has the potential over the long term, to bring about unintended consequences. Some of these consequences include having to go back and complete the entire task again or fix issues that are a result of not applying best our effort. Commitment to continuous improvement breeds excellence. Growing up I often heard my father tell us that no matter the endeavor or job, everyone should know the work done by one of his children because of how well it was done. This was his simple way of teaching us to approach all things with excellence. Excellence does not require perfection. Excellence merely requires giving your very best, determining where improvements can be made, incorporating those improvements and giving more of your best. Always choose excellence.

Monday Morning Minute:

_____

_____

_____

_____

_____

_____

_____

_____

Friday Follow-up:

_____

_____

_____

_____

_____

_____

_____

_____

19

"One tree can start a forest; one smile can begin a friendship; one hand can lift a soul; one candle can wipe out darkness; one laugh can conquer gloom; one hope can raise your spirits; one touch can show you care; one life can make the difference; be that One today." -Author Unknown. Education, job title, income, neighborhood, and the many superficial things we believe are required to make a difference, are actually no indicator of the impact you can have on others, even on the world. Embrace this notion. Your words and actions are powerful. Others need you to show up as proof that THERE IS POWER IN ONE. That one is YOU. One small gesture can mean so much. Be that one today, this week, this month, this year; for yourself, for your family, for your friends, for your work teammates; even for strangers. BE THE ONE.

Monday Morning Minute:

_____

_____

_____

_____

_____

_____

_____

_____

Friday Follow-up:

_____

_____

_____

_____

_____

_____

_____

_____

20

DATE:_____

Take pride in and ownership of your passions, your work and your life. What you DON'T or WON'T do has the potential to set you apart just as much as what you DO or WILL DO. In our personal lives we must take ownership and responsibility for our choices. If we expect to be successful, we must choose the forward motions that lead to the success we seek. Taking personal ownership does not mean doing the job of someone else. It does not mean others should not be held accountable. Personal ownership is all about deciding that success for ALL of us begins with each of us as individual contributors to the greater good. Commit to looking for opportunities to be the solution or fill in the gap when there is a need. Henry Ford said: "If everyone is moving forward, then success takes care of itself.", and Admiral Hyman G. Rickover said, "To complaints of a job poorly done, one often hears the excuse, 'I am not responsible.' I believe that is literally correct. The man who takes such a stand in fact is not responsible; he is irresponsible." Take ownership of your today and your tomorrow.

Monday Morning Minute:

_____

_____

_____

_____

_____

_____

_____

_____

Friday Follow-up:

_____

_____

_____

_____

_____

_____

_____

_____

21

DATE:_____

"Learn to light a candle in the darkest moments of someone's life. Be the light that helps others see; it is what gives life its deepest significance." -Roy T. Bennett. There are days and even moments when we are the only bright spot in another person's life. It is imperative we know how important this may be. It can feel like such a burden when we choose to give grace in our personal and professional lives, however, we don't always know what others are facing. Even those close to us may not have shared problems they are facing. They could have received bad news, had an argument with a family member or friend, or simply have been cut off in traffic causing moments of stress to be carried into their next interaction. The decision to use our light for good could be their saving grace in the moment. Expending the energy to be a shining light can be overwhelming when we already have too much to do and our own issue to face. Still, the opportunity to be the one who lends a hand instead of needing the hand is an opportunity to be a shining light and to be the help that makes a difference. The choice is yours. Be the light!

Monday Morning Minute:

_____

_____

_____

_____

_____

_____

_____

_____

Friday Follow-up:

_____

_____

_____

_____

_____

_____

_____

_____

22

DATE:_____

    "Bitterness is the acid that eats its own container." - Bryan Chapell. All of us have been hurt or wronged in some way by someone. Many times, we hold on to negative emotions and unforgiveness while the offending party has gone on with their daily lives. We suffer alone, often allowing our physical and mental health and even our relationships to be adversely affected. While forgiving may be a difficult proposition, forgiving one who has mistreated you, allows you to freely move forward. Katherine Ponder said it this way: "When you hold resentment toward another, you are bound to that person or condition by an emotional link that is stronger than steel. Forgiveness is the only way to dissolve that link and get free." Choosing forgiveness and refusing to become bitter allows the liberation of the mind and heart from carrying an incredibly heavy burden. Free yourself. FORGIVE!

Monday Morning Minute:

_____

_____

_____

_____

_____

_____

_____

_____

Friday Follow-up:

_____

_____

_____

_____

_____

_____

_____

_____

23

DATE:_____

   "A ship is always safe at shore but that is not what it's built for." – Albert Einstein. Will you be still and simply exist or will you leave the shore? Courage requires a boldness to speak a truth, take a step, admit a fault, say yes or maybe even say no. In courage you must have the willingness to be wrong, make a mistake or fail. Some see courage as a lack of fear. It is not. Although courage does not wipe out fear, it cannot co-exist quietly with fear. Researcher, professor, and speaker Brene' Brown said, "courage is born out of vulnerability, not strength". It seems a contradiction yet rings so true. Think of the people who have made an impact on you. They have walked through their fear and vulnerability, most likely with some discomfort and shown courage. They have pulled the anchor and sailed into the waters whether calm or choppy. Let their examples of courage empower you.

Monday Morning Minute:

_____

_____

_____

_____

_____

_____

_____

_____

Friday Follow-up:

_____

_____

_____

_____

_____

_____

_____

_____

24

DATE:_____

"I don't look to jump over 7-foot bars. I look around for 1-foot bars I can step over." -Warren Buffett. Warren Buffett is one of the richest men alive and also one of the most down to earth and practical men you will ever meet. I've not only heard and read this, but I personally experienced this when I had the great fortune of meeting him as we were both leaving dinner with separate groups at a conference in Omaha, Nebraska where he lives a very modest life for a person who has more money than he could spend in several lifetimes. Pursuing big audacious goals is admirable, however, progress can also be made as a series of smaller wins. It is important to realize you can get over the 7-foot bars by stacking the 1-foot bars of forward progress. Another great leader, Martin Luther King, Jr. said "If you can't fly then run, if you can't run then walk, if you can't walk then crawl, but whatever you do you have to keep moving forward." Fast or slow. One inch or one foot. Keep moving forward.

Monday Morning Minute:

_____

_____

_____

_____

_____

_____

_____

_____

Friday Follow-up:

_____

_____

_____

_____

_____

_____

_____

25

Be the reason someone smiles today. -Unknown. You can change a life, or at least a moment in a life, with just a smile. Each of us has the opportunity and power to bring happiness to the world each day. More importantly, we have the opportunity to bring a little happy to even one life each day which in turn will touch the world. There is a "someone" to make smile in each of our paths today and every day. Your smile may be the only bring spot in someone's day. Earlexia Norwood, MD wrote in the October 5, 2017 Henry Ford Living Well Blog that "Smiling even has health benefits for the smiler. Smiling reduces blood pressure, increases endurance, reduces pain, reduces stress and strengthens the immune system". Be the bright spot. Smile. That small kindness may be just what someone needs. It may not be clear in the moment, but what you do may just be what turns their day around and gives some hope that things will turn out better than they expected. Smile. It will benefit you and others. Be the reason.

Monday Morning Minute:

_____

_____

_____

_____

_____

_____

_____

_____

Friday Follow-up:

_____

_____

_____

_____

_____

_____

_____

_____

26

DATE:_____

"So often in life things that you regard as an impediment turn out to be great good fortune." -Ruth Bader Ginsberg. If each of us thinks back over the challenges we've faced in our lives I am confident most of us can name many times we have come away from a challenge with a positive outcome or at minimum an outcome better than expected. From challenges we many times gain new knowledge, new or improved processes, new strength(s), new or improved relationships, new jobs and so much more. I must admit that it can be pretty difficult in the midst of challenges to see that the long-term result might actually be something good. When I began to personally reflect on this quote and my own life and career, I was inspired and reassured as my list of positives ended up pretty long.

As you begin this new week, I encourage you to take a little time to personally reflect on times when the end result of a challenge has actually turned out to be better than you expected. I also encourage you to remember this quote moving forward and choose to not only see the problem but find the possibilities in tough times.

Monday Morning Minute:

_____

_____

_____

_____

_____

_____

_____

_____

_____

Friday Follow-up:

_____

_____

_____

_____

_____

_____

_____

_____

27

DATE:_____

"Gratitude can transform common days into thanksgivings, turn routine jobs into joy, and change ordinary opportunities into blessings." -William Arthur Ward. Every day can be a sort of Thanksgiving if we adjust our perspective. As we face challenges and changes in our lives or at work, or just simply get tired; I challenge you to pause for a moment of gratitude for just one thing in your life and experience how it changes the course of your day. I read the following passage online and began incorporating it into my daily thought patterns. The impact has been pretty amazing for me personally and I hope it will be the same for you. "Begin the day with an "I GET TO" mentality instead of an "I HAVE TO" thought process... I GET TO go to work. I GET TO have a busy day. Whatever it may be. We often dress our opportunities as stress, but they are in fact blessings." -Author unknown. Who are you grateful you GET TO have in your life—even if they are challenging? What are you grateful that you GET TO do?

Monday Morning Minute:

_____

_____

_____

_____

_____

_____

_____

_____

Friday Follow-up:

_____

_____

_____

_____

_____

_____

_____

_____

28

DATE:_____

    "Times and conditions change so rapidly that we must keep our aim constantly focused on the future." -Walt Disney. In recent years, the term "thought leader" has become a buzz word describing individuals and particularly great leaders who share their knowledge and wisdom and whose views on a subject are taken to be authoritative and influential. Mr. Disney, among his many accomplishments, was a thought leader well before the term was ever coined. This quote spoken many years ago from this business and thought leader has never been more true than today. Our rapidly evolving world has increased to nearly warp speed. While it is critical to develop goals with plans and roadmaps to help keep us focused on accomplishing our goals, we must continue to keep in mind we will always face change based on a myriad of elements both within and external to our span of influence and control. Don't be left behind. Develop plans while still remaining agile enough to adapt to both current and future conditions.

Monday Morning Minute:

_____

_____

_____

_____

_____

_____

_____

_____

Friday Follow-up:

_____

_____

_____

_____

_____

_____

_____

_____

29

"There are better things ahead than any we leave behind." -C.S. Lewis. If you haven't recently thought about your future and formulated a vision for your life, now is the time. To build a clear vision, there is a difficult step that must be taken. That step is letting go of the past. Past failures are not final. Even past successes are just that, THE PAST. Build on both your failures and successes to set the vision for your life. Be intentional. What do you want next? Where do you wish to be in the future? Tom Steyer says, "Clarity of vision is the key to achieving your objectives." Remember, defining your vision is bigger and broader than developing goals. Set goals that will allow you to attain your vision. Spend some quality time with yourself just thinking about your vision. Think big. Bigger than you've imagined in the past.

Monday Morning Minute:

_____

_____

_____

_____

_____

_____

_____

_____

Friday Follow-up:

_____

_____

_____

_____

_____

_____

_____

_____

30

DATE:_____

"Darkness cannot drive out darkness; only light can do that. Hate cannot drive out hate; only love can do that." -Martin Luther King, Jr. We live in a world where chaos, dissension and deliberate disrespect has driven many to live and speak in hate. You are a catalyst for the opposite. As individual citizens of the world we have the power to reverse what we see. If you are not the one marching, you can serve. If you are not on the stage speaking, speak love and kindness to others in your path. If you are not the one legislating, send the message forward to those who do. You may or may not be seen by many, yet you are seen by those around you. In the words of Maya Angelou, "Love recognizes no barriers. It jumps hurdles, leaps fences, penetrates walls to arrive at its destination full of hope." Each day you have the opportunity to bring light and love to everyone you meet. Be the love in your world.

Monday Morning Minute:

_____

_____

_____

_____

_____

_____

_____

Friday Follow-up:

_____

_____

_____

_____

_____

_____

_____

31

DATE:_____

    Joy does not simply happen to us. We have to choose joy and keep choosing it every day. -Henri Nouwen. Consistetnly choosing joy may prove difficult when the cirucmstances of life bring challenges our way. We may experience illness, financial challenge, heartbreak, loss, tough days at work, tough days at home and more, yet the personal decision to make joy a priority can soften the blow in any of these circumstances. Choosing joy does not guarantee evey moment will be happy as there is a difference in deep internal joy and happiness which can be fleeting. Joy encompasses a measure of hope that trancends the momentary ups and downs life may throw our way. Instead of allowing circumstances to get us down we must live in gratitude for what IS right in life and rememebr that joy is a choice. Choose joy!

Monday Morning Minute:

_____

_____

_____

_____

_____

_____

_____

_____

Friday Follow-up:

_____

_____

_____

_____

_____

_____

_____

_____

32

Adversity is life's way of creating strength. Adversity creates challenge, and challenge create change, and change is absolutely necessary for growth. If there is no change and challenge, there can be no growth and development." -Wille Jolley. I will admit that I am one of those persons who would much rather avoid adversity, nearly at all costs, if I could. I am not so lucky as to have avoided adversity throughout my own life. Adversity has facilitated a number of make-or-break moments in my life. To get through some of these moments, I have had to be brave, bold and prepared to speak up when the time arose. The growth created from adversity has the power to be deeper and stronger, built by the stamina you've developed while overcoming the hurdles you've cleared. See adversity as an opportunity to make progress; no matter how big or small that progress may be. The point is that you can overcome any adversity with the right mindset. Embrace adversity for the growth it brings.

Monday Morning Minute:

_____

_____

_____

_____

_____

_____

_____

_____

Friday Follow-up:

_____

_____

_____

_____

_____

_____

_____

_____

33

"If you want to lift yourself up, lift up someone else."– Booker T. Washington. I have heard my father say many times as he has performed his responsibilities as a pastor; when counseling, visiting the sick and comforting those who'd had a loss, that he came away from some of those interactions feeling he had learned something, had a conversation that uplifted his spirit or felt he otherwise benefitted as much or more from the interaction than the person he was there to encourage and support. While I know his care, concern and encouraging words certainly had positive impact on those he served, I have come to appreciate exactly what he meant by this. I did not really understand this when I was much younger, yet as the years have gone by and I have had the opportunity to serve as a leader, this concept has become crystal clear. What we do for others many times has as much of an impact on us as it does them. We encourage, we feel better ourselves. We give, we recognize we are better off than we have acknowledged. We serve, we find strength. Remember to encourage others and in doing so, you just may also encourage yourself.

Monday Morning Minute:

_____

_____

_____

_____

_____

_____

_____

_____

Friday Follow-up:

_____

_____

_____

_____

_____

_____

_____

_____

34

DATE:_____

    Those who play rarely become brittle in the face of stress or lose the healing capacity for humor. -Stuart Brown. The seriousness of life can cause us to forget how to find enjoyment in each day. We work hard, we take care of our families and support our friends. We should also take time to play. Play does not require long vacations, spending hordes of money or any monumental preparation. What play DOES require is finding time to kick around in the leaves in fall, make snow angels in the winter, dig in the dirt in spring, and if you can't get to the beach in the summer, maybe you should create one on the lawn. Sometimes one must forget what others think and remembering to laugh, even, or especially at work. The article, "The Benefits of Play for Adults" in the May 27, 2019, edition of The Beacon from Luminis Health says of play: "It's good for your stress levels. Play can trigger the release of endorphins, the body's feel-good chemicals. These promote an overall sense of wellbeing and can temporarily relieve pain." In my estimation, play keeps us from taking ourselves so seriously, that we lose sight of many important aspects of life. Improve your life. Make time for play.

Monday Morning Minute:

_____

_____

_____

_____

_____

_____

_____

_____

Friday Follow-up:

_____

_____

_____

_____

_____

_____

_____

_____

35

DATE:_____

"At work, or anywhere in life, people should be a team, working for the best of all, not protecting individual egos." -Jay Woodman. When there are many talented people working together, it is inevitable that egos will break through. When things go well, ego and pride many times cause individuals to take credit. When circumstances are tough, we sometimes experience finger pointing or refusal to take responsibility by those who seek the unachievable status of perfection. Great teams share credit for wins and also share the burden of mistakes and failures. View both triumphs and failures as building blocks to excellence. If you are a member of a team or a leader of a team, what you invest is critical to both your performance and the performance of the entire team. Nelson Mandela once said: "I never lose. I either win or I learn." This means we are accountable to ourselves and each other and take responsibility for both wins and lessons. All outcomes, both exciting affirmative and adverse are important in our individual and collective development. Be the best on and for the team.

Monday Morning Minute:

_____

_____

_____

_____

_____

_____

_____

_____

Friday Follow-up:

_____

_____

_____

_____

_____

_____

_____

_____

36

DATE:_____

    Breathe in deeply to bring your mind home to your body. -Thich Nhat Hanh. Regularly practice the art of deep breathing. When excited, breathe. When upset, breathe, and then breathe again. Deep breathing is a natural stress reliever and aids in remaining calm and focused. Taking a moment to inhale and exhale a cleansing breath clears the mind. Taking a deep breath, thinking through not only how you respond, but how you allow the current moment or a person to affect you overall is very important. We face many challenges and sometimes challenging people daily in our personal and professional lives. When these moments come, take a deep breath, and think through your reaction before you speak or allow your facial expression or body language to speak for you. While we can't control every situation and we surely can't control others, we *can* control our own reactions. Remember to breathe in the feeling and breathe out any negativity. Just BREATHE…

Monday Morning Minute:

_____

_____

_____

_____

_____

_____

_____

_____

_____

Friday Follow-up:

_____

_____

_____

_____

_____

_____

_____

_____

_____

37

"True grit is making a decision and standing by it, doing what must be done. No moral man can have peace of mind if he leaves undone what he knows he should have done." -John Wayne. Words like resilience, determination, perseverance, grit... these are just a few words that describe the ability to keep going through tough times. During times of difficulty, we may hear these words daily if not many times each day. Most of us had already experienced some difficult times in our lives, and recent years have piled on more than many of us would have thought we could handle. Yet here we are. Here YOU are. Still here, still going, still taking care of business each day, and taking care of your families, sometimes even your friends, co-workers and many others in your extended circles and communities. Give yourself the pep talk Les Brown referenced in his quote, " You must tell yourself, 'No matter how hard it is, or how hard it gets, I'm going to make it'." Keep tapping into your resilience, your determination, your perseverance, and your grit! You *will* make it!

Monday Morning Minute:

_____

_____

_____

_____

_____

_____

_____

_____

Friday Follow-up:

_____

_____

_____

_____

_____

_____

_____

_____

38

DATE:_____

    Every life is precious. Please treasure each and every day, the present, the moment and yourself. -Ichiga Tochamo. We spend a lot of time rushing from place to place, doing more, achieving the highest accomplishments and amassing more possessions. Yet, many fail to acknowledge being able to physically move around going where you choose, strive for and achieve goals, and make the money to buy what you wish are gifts that all people do not have. It is quite easy to take life and the ability to live and enjoy it for granted. I encourage you to treasure more than the tangible treasures you can measure in dollars or stature. Slow down and take stock. Savor the moment, the sun, flowers blooming, rain that waters those flowers and the grass, relationships with family and friends, even memories of those who are no longer here. Actress Judy Garland once said, "The greatest treasures are those invisible to the eye but found by the heart." Take stock of the real treasures in your life.

Monday Morning Minute:

_____

_____

_____

_____

_____

_____

_____

_____

Friday Follow-up:

_____

_____

_____

_____

_____

_____

_____

_____

39

DATE:_____

"Peace. It does not mean to be in a place where there is no noise, trouble or hard work. It means to be in the midst of those things and still be calm in your heart. -Unknown Most of us are constantly bombarded with information. Nearly twenty-four hours a day we are receiving text messages, emails, data, tweets, posts, timelines, reels and more digitally. This is on top of our "real" daily lives that consist of our family, friends, co-workers and neighbors to name only a few segments of our life ecosystems. Take care to protect your peace. This advice is easy to give and sometimes hard to follow. Peace is mostly predicated on your reaction and response to people and situations. It begins first with a personal commitment to not allowing outside influences to stir up storms inside your mind and heart. "Do not let the behavior of others destroy your inner peace." -Dalai Lama. Commit to keeping your mind, heart and soul at peace.

Monday Morning Minute:

_____

_____

_____

_____

_____

_____

_____

_____

Friday Follow-up:

_____

_____

_____

_____

_____

_____

_____

_____

DATE:_____

"Working through each layer of the self is the key to inner healing." -Vex King. If you've ever watched shows like Design Star on HGTV or Chopped on Food Network, you may have heard the judges advise contestants to "EDIT" their design or dish because there were just too many elements preventing the room or dish to come together as a cohesive finished product. Too many competing styles or flavors can create a sort of "chaos". This same idea must be used in our lives and work to promote healing. Examine your life to determine the people, places and things that don't serve to bring peace or progress to your life; to bring the healing and happiness you seek. Tori Amos says, "Healing takes courage, and we all have courage, even if we have to dig a little to find it." Healing requires embracing who and what is positive and good in and for your life while being courageous enough to let go of what isn't aligned with your values, priorities and peace. The process may be difficult, but the end result is truly worth the effort.

Monday Morning Minute:

_____

_____

_____

_____

_____

_____

_____

_____

Friday Follow-up:

_____

_____

_____

_____

_____

_____

_____

_____

41

"Most of the important things in the world have been accomplished by people who have kept on trying when there seemed to be no hope at all." -Dale Carnegie. Many of these people have done so while smiling when they were not happy and encouraging others while they were struggling themselves. Know this: All of us carry something. Yours might be situations with family, friends, your marriage, your relationship or lack of a relationship, great jobs, not so great jobs that must be kept to pay the bills, businesses or other commitments with many responsibilities that are demanding your time and energy... You get the picture. We ALL carry something. The question is: HOW do you carry YOUR "something"? Even when its heavy enough to bring you to your knees? Do your best to carry yours with grace and have the courage to share your story. You may be just the inspiration someone else needs to maintain their own hope to keep going.

Monday Morning Minute:

_____

_____

_____

_____

_____

_____

_____

_____

Friday Follow-up:

_____

_____

_____

_____

_____

_____

_____

_____

42

"Be that person who roots for others. Who tells a stranger they look amazing and encourages others to believe in themselves and their dreams." -Unknown. It is so easy to look at others and find something wrong or something to criticize. There are many reasons people choose to see not the best but what they consider the worst or the wrong about others. Even great qualities get ridiculed from time to time. This is your challenge to be the one who sees something good in each person you meet. This is your challenge to not just SEE the good but to SPEAK the good. I have found that speaking good into others and speaking well of others lifts me as well. Every day we have the ability to give the gift of good; the chance to add a positive, affirming moment to the lives of others. This ability and choice also requires some humility; the understanding that we too are imperfect and it is those around us and sometimes even strangers who have been the ones to speak the good into us when we most needed. Be the one to speak the good.

Monday Morning Minute:

_____

_____

_____

_____

_____

_____

_____

_____

Friday Follow-up:

_____

_____

_____

_____

_____

_____

_____

_____

43

DATE:_____

"I've missed more than 9,000 shots in my career. I've lost almost 300 games. 26 times, I've been trusted to take the game winning shot and missed. I've failed over and over and over again in my life. And that is why I succeed." -Michael Jordan. I personally love hearing words of wisdom from those who have worked hard and fought to be great; those who never stopped going for their goals and driving toward their dreams. Missteps included, to keep going is the ultimate indicator of eventual or ongoing success. It is even more motivating when I think upon all I have seen ordinary people accomplish. On many occasions we are able to cheer a success and other times challenges can nearly knock us down. Still, we keep going, knowing that we must persevere beyond the immediate moment. You are an example of continuing to move forward despite how many triumphs or trials you face. Ed Latimore speaks of motivation this way, "Motivated people always find a way. Unmotivated people always find a way not to." How are you motivated to keep going?

Monday Morning Minute:

_____

_____

_____

_____

_____

_____

_____

_____

Friday Follow-up:

_____

_____

_____

_____

_____

_____

_____

_____

44

"Show respect even to people who don't deserve it; not as a reflection of their character, but as a reflection of yours." -Dave Willis. You may know the lyrics of the Aretha Franklin song, 'Respect". She sang, "R-E-S-P-E-C-T, find out what it means to me". This song has always resonated with me because everyone wants respect and so many of us are easily triggered when we feel disrespected. When it comes to respect, don't just look for respect from others but commit to being responsible for your actions and words. How you interact with and respond to others truly is a conscious choice. Showing respect may set an example that ultimately helps others to make a change for the better. Even if it does not, you will be able to respect yourself more for having done the right thing.

R-E-S-P-E-C-T... What does it mean to you?

Monday Morning Minute:

_____

_____

_____

_____

_____

_____

_____

_____

_____

Friday Follow-up:

_____

_____

_____

_____

_____

_____

_____

_____

_____

45

"Falling down is how we grow. Staying down is how we die." -Brian Vaszily. Failures may detour us, and whether you believe it or not, sometimes they elevate us in the long run. Do not allow failures to define you. Do not let them deter you from your purpose. While you're getting up from the "fall" of a failure, look up and learn. Whatever you do, you can't stay down. Get up. Keep putting one foot in front or the other and move forward. Keep the lesson but kill the urge to allow defeat to define you. Some of the most well-known and successful names we know are clear examples of learning from failures and getting better as a result. Ludwig Beethoven, Albert Einstein, Thomas Edison, Steven Spielberg Oprah Winfrey, Michael Jordan; J.K. Rowling and Bill Gates are just a few who had one or more failures that they could have allowed to define them but each of them kept going until they succeeded. I too know this experience personally. One job I really wanted but was not hired for many years ago, left me open for the role that became the foundation of my future career path; a career far better than I had initially planned for myself. When things don't go as planned, remember the Japanese proverb: "Fall down seven times. Get up eight."

Monday Morning Minute:

_____

_____

_____

_____

_____

_____

_____

_____

Friday Follow-up:

_____

_____

_____

_____

_____

_____

_____

_____

46

"There is virtue in work and there is virtue in rest. Use both and overlook neither." -Alan Cohen. To be the super achiever you most likely are, you must also learn to balance the hustle and bustle with rest and rejuvenation. This also requires making the conscious choice about what you will say yes or no to. To achieve balance, planning for rest and energy replenishment is critical. If you are already practicing the balanced life, celebrate yourself and commit to continue. If you are still "burning the candle at both ends" as the saying goes, I challenge you to take the time to build your rest plan. While sleep is a part of the total equation, sleep alone does not equate to rest. The Merriam-Webster dictionary defines rest this way: "to relax, sleep or refrain from taking part in work or an activity". A rest plan might include, in addition to sleep, spending time with no technology, taking time to sit and listen to relaxing music, taking a leisurely walk, taking a long bath, relaxing near water or making time watch and enjoy the sunrise or sunset. Remember Eleanor Brown's words, "Rest and self-care are so important. When you take time to replenish your spirit, it allows you to serve others from the overflow. You cannot serve from an empty vessel". Relax, rejuvenate, REST.

Monday Morning Minute:

_____

_____

_____

_____

_____

_____

_____

_____

Friday Follow-up:

_____

_____

_____

_____

_____

_____

_____

_____

47

Our thoughts are extremely powerful. Henry Ford said, "Whether you think you can, or you think you can't – you're right". Think of those days you start with gratitude and positive thoughts about what you will accomplish. Those are the days that usually turn out best. Then think of those days you begin with doubt or dread and how those days many times don't turn out so well. The days I start with a resolve that I can get through my to do list and meet every challenge, are the days I solve the most problems and accomplish the most good. The days I let doubt and fear of failure creep in, are the days that end with just as much stress as at the start of the day. I openly share my own experiences because in our humanity, we have a lot in common. You likely also have days, projects; even goals you start with positive thoughts and enthusiasm and some you start with worry and concern. Again, this is human, yet let this be the reminder that our thoughts *can* be, and most times *will* be the driving force in our outcomes. Keep a positive mindset.

Monday Morning Minute:

_____

_____

_____

_____

_____

_____

_____

_____

Friday Follow-up:

_____

_____

_____

_____

_____

_____

_____

_____

48

DATE:_____

"You can do anything if you put your mind to it, the only thing that can stop you is yourself." -Unknown. "You can do anything." I heard these words from my parents from a very early age. I then heard it from teachers, adults in my church then my sister and brothers. I've said those words to my sons and my grandson more times than I could ever begin to count. I hope that you have both heard and believed that you can do anything throughout your life. If you haven't, I'm telling you today. You can do ANYTHING! You must also know it's never too late. My mother earned her PhD at sixty eight. What is that anything you've wanted to do? You CAN do it! It's critical that you not see any limitations on what you can do when you make up your mind. You alone have the power to do anything you put your mind to. What is that thing you want to do? What is that hurdle you need to jump over? Start with your mindset about it, document your plan, even if it's a simple thing or dust off the plan you already have and take the first step forward. You CAN do ANYTHING!

Monday Morning Minute:

_____

_____

_____

_____

_____

_____

_____

_____

Friday Follow-up:

_____

_____

_____

_____

_____

_____

_____

_____

49

DATE:_____

"Self-control is strength. Calmness is mastery. You have to get to the point where your mood doesn't shift based on insignificant actions of someone else. Don't allow others to control the direction of your life. Don't allow your emotions to overpower your intelligence." -Unknown. I frequently come across this quote online and each time I read it, it is a simple yet bold reminder that my reaction to people and situations can be critical to the final outcome of a situation and to my own well-being. It also brings me back to a few years ago when I had a leadership coach who helped me to assess how I reacted in high stake situations. The reflections were quite eye-opening to say the least. The coach helped me to create a series of questions to ask myself while taking that deep breath during difficult conversations or when the room was "charged". The questions related to how I felt at the moment, why I felt a particular way and what my response should be. The final question I was to ask myself, "Is this the hill you want to die on?"; meaning how far do you really want to go and how do you make your point in a manner that you will feel good about later, especially if it is has the potential of damaging your current position, career or even a relationship? This is the question that most often comes to mind when I contemplate my reaction. Prasad Mohes says it like this: "The mind is like water. When it's turbulent, it's difficult to see. When it's calm, everything becomes clear." Calm your mind before you calculate your response.

Monday Morning Minute:

_____

_____

_____

_____

_____

_____

_____

Friday Follow-up:

_____

_____

_____

_____

_____

_____

_____

50

"Unease, anxiety, tension, stress, worry— all forms of fear— are caused by too much future, and not enough presence. Guilt, regret, resentment, grievances, sadness, bitterness and all forms of non-forgiveness are caused by too much past and not enough presence." -Eckhart Tolle There is great importance in planning and preparing for the future. There is equally great importance in learning from the past. What is even more critical for each of us, is to ensure that neither worrying about the future or living in the past (bad or good) cripples us today. We see a myriad of circumstances bombarding us today including international war, our country at odds within itself over inane, ironically a descriptor awfully close to insane, issues like race, religion and political affiliations. Jonah Leher puts it this way: "We need spaces that surprise us. Because it is the exchanges we don't expect, with the people we just met, that will change the way we think about everything." To be open to these opportunities, surprise moments of joy, you must be present in today. Despite the past, even just yesterday, despite what may come in the future, choose to live in the good you find today. The choice is yours alone.

Monday Morning Minute:

_____

_____

_____

_____

_____

_____

_____

_____

Friday Follow-up:

_____

_____

_____

_____

_____

_____

_____

51

Oxford Languages defines sanctuary as "a place of refuge or safety". With all that is happening in the world at large and in our personal and professional lives, I encourage you to claim your own space of sanctuary. The place you claim may be physical or it might possibly be spiritual or mental. Just be sure to claim the space. I also encourage you to help those around you by being a place of sanctuary. When there is chaos all around, be the calm. When there are storms, be security. Even when all is right with the world, just be there to witness the sigh of relief and the reminder that it's ok to soak up the good. Take care of yourself. Take care of eithers. Claim sanctuary. BE sanctuary.

Monday Morning Minute:

_____

_____

_____

_____

_____

_____

_____

Friday Follow-up:

_____

_____

_____

_____

_____

_____

_____

52

"Perfection is not attainable, but if we chase perfection, we can catch excellence." -Vince Lombardi. Excellence as defined by Oxford Languages is the quality of being outstanding or extremely good. I submit to you that in all endeavors we should strive to operate in excellence. I was taught that average is not an option and to put my very best into anything I set out to do; even what seemed to be the most menial tasks. Growing up, even cleaning the brass and crystal teardrop chandelier was a serious and detailed process. Getting an A in each class was important in my family, still the way in which the work was approached was just as important as the actual grade. Consistent excellence is a journey. It can be quite easy to slip into taking the short path rather than the long road or only operating in excellence when it will be noticed by someone we deem important. Don't be fooled. Someone is always there watching and needing to see you giving your best effort and demonstrating excellence. Live, act, work in excellence.

Monday Morning Minute:

_____

_____

_____

_____

_____

_____

_____

_____

Friday Follow-up:

_____

_____

_____

_____

_____

_____

_____

_____

About the Author
Sonja W. Bachus

Sonja W. Bachus is a healthcare executive with twenty years of operations and leadership experience serving in Federally Qualified Health Centers and large hospital systems. Sonja is a transformational leader with a passion and love for people and helping others reach their potential and dreams. Her strong spiritual foundation informs her authenticity and commitment to leading with love and grace.

Sonja's core "love leadership" belief is that a foundation of love, coupled with strong accountability brings out the best in people and results in performance excellence and accomplishing operational and financial goals.

She also is the principal/owner of DND Management Co. aka sonjawbachus.com, an executive coaching and leadership development practice. Sonja holds a Bachelor of Business Administration from Washburn University, Topeka, KS, and a Master of Jurisprudence in Health Law from Loyola University Chicago Law School and is a Community Health Center Executive Fellow. She has two adult sons and four grandchildren.